ART THAT BEGETS ART

CALEB MONROE

"Art That Begets Art" copyright © 2022 by J. Caleb Monroe
Cover design copyright © 2022 by J. Caleb Monroe
Psithurism Press logo copyright © by shutter2u

All rights reserved.

No part of this book may be reproduced in any form or by any electronic or mechanical means, including information storage and retrieval systems, without written permission from the author, except for the use of brief quotations in a book review.

Scriptures taken from the Holy Bible, New International Version®, NIV®. Copyright © 1973, 1978, 1984, 2011 by Biblica, Inc.™ Used by permission of Zondervan. All rights reserved worldwide. www.zondervan.com The "NIV" and "New International Version" are trademarks registered in the United States Patent and Trademark Office by Biblica, Inc.™

For Sean

ART THAT BEGETS ART

CONTENTS

1. Creation   1
2. Community   5
3. Case Study   9

Acknowledgments   13
About the Author   15
Mary's Story   17

1

CREATION

Scripture begins with the Spirit of God hovering over the welter and waste of the darkness of the deep. Then God said "Let there be light," creating the the medium of sound and generating the possibility of every auditory art that ever has or ever will exist, from music to rhetoric,

while also creating the medium of sight and generating the possibility of every visual art that ever has or ever will exist, from cave paintings to virtual reality.

When God observed these creations and declared them good—not just good, but good to the eyes—God introduced the concepts of aesthetics, skill, proficiency, craftsmanship, rightness, and even morality as intrinsic to creation and to the creative act. Concepts we can summarize in three words—truth, goodness, and beauty.

Which are also, by the way, names for the second person of the Trinity. Dostoyevsky was being incredibly accurate when he wrote, "Beauty will save the world."

Next, God created time as a container in which that first darkness and that first light would interact and proceeded to place conscious beings—*us*—within it. Placing consciousness in time created narrative, generating the possibility of every literary art that ever has or ever will exist, from journalism to screenwriting.

Those conscious beings were created specifically to portray God's likeness, generating the possibility of every performance art that ever has or ever will exist, from dance to acting.

What's more, these living portrayals were crafted from solid matter. In fact, this entire tale is one of the intangible becoming tangible—generating the possibility of every physical art that ever has or ever will exist, from painting to carpentry.

Speaking of physical arts, God "formed" Adam from earth—that verb is a sculpting term. God "built" Eve—the verb there is an architectural term. The next human, Cain, was given a name derived from a metalworking verb. See, God doesn't just create new things. God creates new *ways* of creating new things, generating the possibility of every yet-unimagined art form still to come in the lifespan of the universe.

And it was here—right here—in the midst of this mind-boggling something-from-nothing cosmic storm of creativity, long before sin ever entered the picture, that God created work. In a single sentence, humans are assigned the fields of reproduction, multiplication, replenishment, mastery, and governance, generating the possibility of every vocation that ever has or ever will exist. God entwined work and creativity from the beginning of both. Art as work and work as art comprise part of the DNA of the universe.

There is, unfortunately, more to the story. The humans took their built-in drive to create new things and used it to conceive of something radically and rebelliously new—they imagined autonomy from God, generating the possibility of every sin that ever has or ever will exist, from comparison to murder.

And since God is life, this attempt at autonomy from the divine created separation from life, generating the certainty of every death that ever has or ever will take place, from yours to mine.

The advent of sin and death disfigured both work and creativity. They became difficult. They became labor. Opportunities to worship the wrong things. Means to survive death as long as possible. Tools of oppression and building blocks for systems that devalue, wound, distort, and kill.

But sin does not get the last word in the story. Not even in the story of its own creation.

The humans responded to their sin by using the possibility of every physical art that had been built into the universe to create the first physical things not made directly by God. Their motivation was shame, but that couldn't remove the God-images they were so, even though it was an act of sinful cover-up, they created clothing, generating the possibility of every fashion art that ever has or ever will exist, from weaving and dying to design.

Then God came along and, even deeply betrayed, redeemed the humans' creative work—created a better version of what they had made—generating the possibility that any and every work we do can be made better by God. Can be redeemed. Can be an act of repair.

Creative work was made as a goodness and still retains that good. But in a fallen world the role of that goodness changes. No longer entire goodness on top of entire goodness, it becomes *tikkun olam*, a Hebraic term meaning "world repair." Creative work becomes a way of preserving and reweaving a universe now warped toward entropy.

Work and art now inhabit an inescapable tension. The painter Eric Fischl once remarked that the four traditional roles of artists are describing the Garden, the Fall, Heaven, and Hell. Or: what's right in the world, what's wrong in the world, how it can get better, and how it can get worse.

Only a couple paragraphs after the introduction of that third human, Cain, comes the introduction of another two figures: Jubal, "the father of all those who play the lyre and pipe," and

Tubal-cain, "the forger of all instruments of bronze and iron." Of course, one of the most universal and enduring instruments of bronze or iron ever created is the sword. These, then, are the poles of the tension we now navigate: right and better on one hand, wrong and worse on the other.

The song and the sword.

2

COMMUNITY

Now let's go back a moment to that Spirit hovering over the chaos before everything was kicked off by the creation of light and sound.

The first person in Scripture described as filled with that Spirit of God is the artist Bezalel, commissioned as the foreman and chief artisan for building the Tabernacle. The Tabernacle was many things, but one of the main things was a beautiful work of art, designed by God and commissioned from human artists.

Bezalel's gift from God was actually two-fold: God filled him with the ability to make beauty and "work in all kinds of arts and crafts," and God filled him with "the ability to teach others."

This next bit is crucial: Bezalel was not called alone. Called alongside him was Oholiab, another man given the skill to work in all kinds of arts and crafts and given the ability to teach. No one is called alone. You are not called alone. We live in a society that values the individual above all else, so we tend to read the Bible's use of the pronoun "you" as singular. But most of those "yous" are plural.

God does not rescue us into being individual persons of God. God rescues us into being the people of God. Singular. Together.

Called alongside. It's kind of a reverse individualism. As Peter puts it, "Once you were not a people, but now you are the people of God."

If God has called you as a filmmaker, God has not called you alone. You have been called to filmmaking alongside tens of thousands of others from all backgrounds and walks of life from around the globe. You won't work with most of them but you'll work with many of them and, whether you meet or not, you will all be working toward the goal of filling the world with more and better visual stories. It's the same if you're a designer, musician, sculptor, marketer, cook, parent, mechanic, or farmhand.

Bezalel and Oholiab's together-calling didn't end with them. Their artistic gifts were paired with teaching gifts so they could raise up an entire community of skilled artists. The Tabernacle, blueprinted by none other than God, was intended as a community project. The entire people of God were to participate.

God calls you not only to a craft or an artform. God calls you to a community. God calls you and everyone else in your field to that vocation together. Makes you a people.

And the person working next to you who may not believe in God is no less called than you. They have the same vocation you do. The expressions of your work will probably be different, but your callings are alike.

To illustrate my point, let's look at the Temple. The Tabernacle was a moveable home for God because the people of Israel were nomadic and wandered the desert. Once they were settled in the promised land and ruled by the great king David, David was given God's next and last blueprint for a physical work of art that we know of: the designs for a successor and supercessor to the Tabernacle— a Temple. God asked the people of Israel to build God a permanent home even as God had given them a permanent home. A house into which God invited people and in which people visited with God. God moved in next door.

But this time God did not choose a God-follower to oversee

the project, as had been done with Bezalel. God chose Huramabi, a Phoenician from Tyre who would have worshipped Melqart, Ba'al, and Astarte, some of the most pernicious and reviled false gods in the Hebrew scriptures.

Year later, when that Temple was being rebuilt after being destroyed in the Babylonian invasion, God chose the God-follower Zerubbabel for the task.

But after Jerusalem fell to Pompey, the final version of the Temple—the version in which Jesus himself would walk and minister—was rebuilt under the supervision of Herod the First, a man who worshipped himself with a zeal that led to mass murder and attempted deicide. Still, Jesus defended that Temple as his Father's house to the point of physically attacking those who would defile it.

The artistry and construction of God's own house was overseen as much by those who didn't follow God as those who did.

Creativity, work, and art are not, by any stretch of the imagination that we all have in common, the exclusive domain of Christians. They are divine gifts of grace to all humanity for the expression of God's beautiful and provisional goodness. You are called to your field and made a community with everyone in it by divine sovereignty for the articulation of God's own grand, glorious, and—frankly—mysterious goodness at work in the world.

Which is not to say there are not things which set you apart and make you distinct. After all, only a community full of robust diversity working together can be considered truly unified. Otherwise, it's just uniform.

Scripture tells us a significant distinction is that the current temple is God's people. Plural. We are the house, the space, the artform into which God invites people and in which people visit with God. Through divine, unearned, mind-boggling grace— and grace alone—we are the house where the Spirit of God dwells. We are all Bezalels. In fact, the only direct line of dialogue given to the Holy Spirit in all of Scripture is expressed through our collective mouth.

Think about that for a moment.

That same Holy Spirit who hovered over creation, who inspired Scripture through human authors, who overshadowed Mary and incarnated God as Jesus through her, who renews the face of the earth...That's the same Holy Spirit who dwells in you, whose dialogue is on your lips, and who will actively co-create with you if you participate.

Immediately before that line of dialogue, Scripture describes the total healing of reality and restoration of all things in the most elegant, extravagant terms. A universe made whole, a generative existence saturated with beauty.

And it's a universe in which work still exists. Reproduction, multiplication, replenishment, mastery, and governance. Our work is suspended in tensions now, but the act of—and goodness of—work will long outlive the sin that mars it now.

Work, including creative work, is therefore not the absence of perfection, but a presence—a concrete expression of God's goodness and provision. It is the primary way God chooses to provide for us. For everyone. God could shower us all with manna, always and forever. Instead, God chooses for us to grow and harvest grain and learn to bake bread. For us to work. Interdependently. Because work is *tikkun olam*. It is one of the ways God heals the universe. And God wants us to play an active role in that healing.

3

CASE STUDY

NOW THAT WE'VE TAKEN A BRIEF—INCREDIBLY BRIEF—GLANCE AT some of God's purposes for creative work, let's close by examining some of the ways this played out in a single human life—Mary of Nazareth, perhaps the Bible's best example of what it looks like to join God in God's creative work, rather than merely inviting God into ours.

Just as Bezalel was the first person in Scripture filled with the Holy Spirit, Mary was the first person in Scripture filled by the Christ. And how did she receive this once-in-reality opportunity?

Mary responded with humility.

Told the Holy Spirit would make something unprecedented through her, she humbly agreed to participate.

Mary responded with obedience.

She was probably 13 or 14 years old, and no doubt had a plan for her life. I guarantee it did not include giving birth to God. But she said yes anyway. As artists, visioneers, and professional storytellers, we have a particularly strong tendency to imagine the future of our own stories. Are you willing to give that up?

Mary responded by dying to herself.

And I don't simply mean the phrase metaphorically, as we're

used to hearing it. To be pregnant out of wedlock in that culture at that time was a crime that carried the death penalty. She was young, she was vulnerable, and she was very aware there was a good chance that her yes to God might be how she would die.

Mary responded with service.

Immediately after her conversation with the angel and conceiving through the Holy Spirit, she takes a long and rather dangerous trip to take care of an elderly relative who was also pregnant—undoubtedly a difficult pregnancy, considering her advanced years. Mary, who could genuinely be considered the center of the universe at that point in time, took care of someone else.

I had the privilege of spending some time with an artist whose practice was making icons for Eastern Orthodox churches. This is a practice absolutely saturated in prayer and the overshadowing of the Holy Spirit. I asked her how she prepared for a day doing that kind of work, and her answer was that she would scrub the kitchen floor or give her mom, who had Alzheimer's, a bath. Service was how she spiritually prepared to create beauty.

Mary responded with community.

She was there to serve Elizabeth, yes, but she was also there to share in the community created by a shared vocation. In this case, the vocation of miraculous pregnancy. Mary created a second-half-of-the-conversation space.

When I'm around other writers, I spend the first half of the conversation explaining what it's like to be a Christian. When I'm around other Christians, I spend the first half of the conversation explaining what it's like to be a writer. But when I'm around someone who's both, I can jump to the second half of the conversation, and I've noticed that's where the biggest pockets of encouragement (literally "wrapping in courage") tend to be.

Mary and Elizabeth could jump to the second half of a *very* unique conversation. Could wrap each other in particular, peculiar courage. Like Bezalel and Oholiab—and us—they had not been called alone.

Mary believed in the significance of her insignificance.

She was young, poor, and vulnerable. She lived on the margins of society even before this pregnancy. But she absolutely accepted that's the kind of place where God works. God has always been most active at the margins of society. It's the exact opposite of marginalization—for God, the margin is the center. Not to conflate society and the world at large too much with your particular disciple, but have you found or do you find yourself on the margins of your chosen field? That's rich soil.

God chooses the margin. God *prefers* the margin.

Mary accepted rejection.

She accepted being stigmatized as an adulteress and shunned by those she was closest to. Becoming a social outcast. And even after giving birth and getting married, she would experience the ultimate rejection of being forced to flee her homeland in fear for her own life and those of her family.

As artists, even successful ones, you will face more rejection than success. But this rejection, this unmet intent, this unfulfilled desire, is a place to identify with God, who created an artistic masterpiece—creation itself—then was rejected and saw that masterpiece devalued, abused, and spoiled. God's good desire that none shall perish will not come to pass. God the human died rejected and despised.

Our rejection is a place where we can learn to be like God.

Mary responded with art.

She composed a song, one of the most recited songs in human history, as a container for her experience. She did it working within a genre and artistic tradition, drawing heavily upon the Psalms.

And her art begat art. When John the Baptist was born, Zechariah, who had just spent three months sharing a house with the songwriting Mary, composes a song of his own. I don't think that's an accident. And these are the only two songs in the New Testament until we get to Revelation. Which many believe was written by the same John the Apostle who took Mary home to live with him after Jesus' death.

It's possible that every song in the New Testament comes from either Mary or someone who lived with her.

And that's only the beginning. John's revelation was the first great poem of Christianity and the headwaters of a poetic tradition that produced Dante's *Divine Comedy*, Milton's *Paradise Lost*, Blake's *Jerusalem*, and Eliot's *Four Quartets*. Mary responded to God's creative birthing work in her with creative work of her own that birthed more creative work. Birthed—hundreds and thousands of years later—some of the greatest creative work in human history.

Humility. Obedience. Death. Service. Community. Insignificance. Rejection. Art that begets art.

May we respond likewise.

Amen.

ACKNOWLEDGMENTS

Thank you to Steve Lindsey and the Center for Faith and Work LA for putting on and allowing me to help plan the event at which I gave the speech this essay is adapted from. And to Erin Batali, Sean Johnson, Karen Covell, and Dean Batali, who all encouraged me to do something further with it.

I'm immeasurably grateful to the entire staff of Reality Church of Los Angeles for the best work environment I've ever experienced and for giving me the opportunity to explore these topics professionally.

ABOUT THE AUTHOR

J. Caleb Monroe is the Work and Culture Director at Reality Church of Los Angeles.

He authors comics, movies, and fiction as Caleb Monroe and has written such comics and graphic novels as *Hunter's Fortune*, *Cloaks*, *Batman 80-Page Giant*, *Dawn of the Planet of the Apes: Contagion*, the cult spy-fi classic *Steed and Mrs. Peel.*, and such all ages titles as *Ice Age* and *Peanuts*.

He cowrote the action film *The Mongolian Connection* with director Drew Thomas and his short fiction has appeared in *Athena Voltaire Pulp Tales* and *Leading Edge* magazine, among others.

Caleb periodically lives and writes in Los Angeles. You can visit him at jcalebmonroe.com.

MARY'S STORY
LUKE 1:26-56

In the sixth month of Elizabeth's pregnancy, God sent the angel Gabriel to Nazareth, a town in Galilee, to a virgin pledged to be married to a man named Joseph, a descendant of David. The virgin's name was Mary. The angel went to her and said, "Greetings, you who are highly favored! The Lord is with you."

Mary was greatly troubled at his words and wondered what kind of greeting this might be. But the angel said to her, "Do not be afraid, Mary; you have found favor with God. You will conceive and give birth to a son, and you are to call him Jesus. He will be great and will be called the Son of the Most High. The Lord God will give him the throne of his father David, and he will reign over Jacob's descendants forever; his kingdom will never end."

"How will this be," Mary asked the angel, "since I am a virgin?"

The angel answered, "The Holy Spirit will come on you, and the power of the Most High will overshadow you. So the holy one to be born will be called the Son of God. Even Elizabeth your relative is going to have a child in her old age, and she who was said to be unable to conceive is in her sixth month. For no word from God will ever fail."

"I am the Lord's servant," Mary answered. "May your word to me be fulfilled." Then the angel left her.

At that time Mary got ready and hurried to a town in the hill country of Judea, where she entered Zechariah's home and greeted Elizabeth. When Elizabeth heard Mary's greeting, the baby leaped in her womb, and Elizabeth was filled with the Holy Spirit. In a loud voice she exclaimed: "Blessed are you among women, and blessed is the child you will bear! But why am I so favored, that the mother of my Lord should come to me? As soon as the sound of your greeting reached my ears, the baby in my womb leaped for joy. Blessed is she who has believed that the Lord would fulfill his promises to her!"

And Mary said:

> *"My soul glorifies the Lord*
>   *and my spirit rejoices in God my Savior,*
> *for he has been mindful*
>   *of the humble state of his servant.*
> *From now on all generations will call me blessed,*
>   *for the Mighty One has done great things for me—*
>   *holy is his name.*
> *His mercy extends to those who fear him,*
>   *from generation to generation.*
> *He has performed mighty deeds with his arm;*
>   *he has scattered those who are proud in their inmost*
>   *thoughts.*
> *He has brought down rulers from their thrones*
>   *but has lifted up the humble.*
> *He has filled the hungry with good things*
>   *but has sent the rich away empty.*
> *He has helped his servant Israel,*
>   *remembering to be merciful*
> *to Abraham and his descendants forever,*
>   *just as he promised our ancestors."*

Mary stayed with Elizabeth for about three months and then returned home.

Printed in Great Britain
by Amazon